A

PERSONAL

JOURNAL

RUNNING PRESS
Philadelphia, Pennsylvania

International representatives: Worldwide Media Services, Inc.,
115 East Twenty-third Street, New York, New York 10010.
Canadian representatives: General Publishing Co., Ltd.,
30 Lesmill Road, Don Mills, Ontario M3B 2T6.

9 8 7 6 5 4 3 2 1
Digit on the right indicates the number of this printing.

ISBN 1–56138–117–9

Cover illustration: Eileen Goodman, *Hydrangea Bouquet,* 1990.
Watercolor, 26×40″.
Courtesy Marian Locks Gallery, Philadelphia.

Cover design by Toby Schmidt
Interior design by Nancy Loggins
Picture research by Gillian Speeth
Editing and text research by Melissa Stein
Additional text research by Joan McIntosh
Typography ITC Garamond Light by Commcor
Communications Corporation, Philadelphia, Pennsylvania
Printed in Hong Kong

This book may be ordered by mail from the publisher. Please add $2.50 for postage
and handling. *But try your bookstore first!*

Running Press Book Publishers, 125 South Twenty-second Street,
Philadelphia, Pennsylvania 19103.

GEORGIA O'KEEFFE

American

Poppy

1927

oil on canvas

I LOOK

BACK

AND

REALIZE

THAT

SOMEHOW

I HAVE

MOVED

INTO

THE

FUTURE.

MELODIE BEATTIE
20TH-CENTURY AMERICAN WRITER

TIME TAKES HOLD OF US LIKE A DRAFT

UPWARD, DRAWING AT THE HEATS

IN THE BELLY, IN THE BRAIN . . .

ADRIENNE RICH, B. 1929
AMERICAN POET

THE EVENTS
IN OUR LIVES
HAPPEN IN
A SEQUENCE
IN TIME, BUT
IN THEIR
SIGNIFICANCE
TO OURSELVES,
THEY FIND
THEIR OWN
ORDER . . . THE
CONTINUOUS
THREAD OF
REVELATION.

EUDORA WELTY, B. 1909
AMERICAN WRITER

IRENE RICE PEREIRA

American

Pillar of Fire

1955

oil on canvas

EACH DAY . . . HAS A RARITY . . . .

I COULD PUT IT IN A VASE AND ADMIRE IT,

LIKE THE FIRST DANDELIONS . . .

MARGARET LAURENCE, B. 1926
CANADIAN WRITER

TODAY

IS ALWAYS

HERE. . . .

TOMORROW,

NEVER.

TONI MORRISON, B. 1931
AMERICAN WRITER AND EDUCATOR

. . . THIS IS

REAL LIFE.

JUST

BECAUSE

IT'S ALL

GOING

YOUR WAY

TONIGHT

DOESN'T

MEAN

THAT

TOMORROW

WON'T BRING

SURPRISES.

SO COUNT

YOUR

BLESSINGS

AND

BE HAPPY.

JUDY BLUME, B. 1938
AMERICAN WRITER

Would You Be an Angel?

1989

oil on canvas

TIME WILL OUTWEIGH THE MOMENT.

DEMI MOORE, B. 1962
AMERICAN ACTRESS

SUSAN HEADLEY VAN CAMPEN

American

Black Hollyhocks in Mimi's Glass

1990

watercolor

THERE IS TIME FOR WORK.

AND TIME FOR LOVE.

THAT LEAVES NO OTHER TIME!

GABRIELLE "COCO" CHANEL (1883–1971)
FRENCH FASHION DESIGNER

WHOEVER

LIVES

TRUE

LIFE

WILL

LOVE

TRUE

LOVE . . . .

ELIZABETH BARRETT BROWNING (1806–1861)
ENGLISH POET

THIS LOVE IS IN THE EYES,

NOT YET IN THE HEART'S RANGE....

MAY SARTON, B. 1912
AMERICAN POET

Sita and Sarita

1893–4

oil

IN

LOVE

THERE

ARE

TWO

THINGS:

BODIES

AND

WORDS.

JOYCE CAROL OATES, B. 1938
AMERICAN WRITER AND CRITIC

BODIES CANNOT LIE.

AGNES DE MILLE, B. 1905
AMERICAN DANCER AND CHOREOGRAPHER

A PERSON MIGHT BE PART OF YOU,

ALMOST PART OF YOUR BODY,

AND YET ONCE YOU WENT AWAY FROM THEM

THEY MIGHT UTTERLY CEASE TO BE.

ELIZABETH BOWEN (1899–1973)
IRISH-BORN ENGLISH WRITER

Bacchus #3

1978

acrylic on canvas

PEOPLE IN LOVE . . .

GIVE AWAY

THE SHORT CUTS

TO EVERYBODY'S

SECRETS.

EUDORA WELTY, B. 1909
AMERICAN WRITER

Hydrangea Bouquet

1990

watercolor

. . . THE

LIFE

AND LOVE

OF THE

BODY

IS A

NOBLE

THING,

AGAINST

WHICH

THE

INTELLECT

AND THE

SPIRIT

NEED NOT

WAGE WAR.

MICHELE ROBERTS, B. 1949
ENGLISH WRITER

GENIUS IS ANOTHER WORD FOR MAGIC,

AND THE WHOLE POINT OF MAGIC

IS THAT IT IS INEXPLICABLE.

MARGOT FONTEYN (1919–1991)
AMERICAN WRITER

IF YOUR HEAD TELLS YOU ONE THING

AND YOUR HEART TELLS YOU ANOTHER,

BEFORE YOU DO ANYTHING,

YOU SHOULD FIRST DECIDE WHETHER

YOU HAVE A BETTER HEAD OR A BETTER HEART.

MARILYN VOS SAVANT, B. 1947
AMERICAN WRITER

ELISSA DORFMAN

American

Self-Portrait

1975

oil on canvas

MY MIND AND BODY ARE GOING IN THE SAME DIRECTION

BUT NOT AT THE SAME SPEED.

MARGARET RANDALL, B. 1936
AMERICAN POET

I

PROMISE

TO HOLD

YOU

IN THE

MIND

AS A CUPPED

HAND

PROTECTS

A FLAME.

Marge Piercy, b. 1936
American poet

THEN I DID NOT KNOW

ANY LONGER THAT EARTH

AND SKY WERE EARTH AND SKY.

THE UNIVERSE BREATHED IN AND OUT

AND I DISSOLVED IN IT,

NO LONGER I.

MICHELE ROBERTS, B. 1949
ENGLISH WRITER

P.T. FORRESTER
American

Heavy Heads

1991

watercolor

A PLACE
BELONGS
TO WHOEVER
CLAIMS IT
HARDEST,
REMEMBERS
IT MOST
OBSESSIVELY,
WRENCHES IT
FROM
ITSELF,
SHAPES IT,
RENDERS IT,
LOVES IT
SO RADICALLY
THAT
HE REALLY
MAKES IT
IN HIS
IMAGE.

JOAN DIDION, B. 1934
AMERICAN WRITER

ELAINE NORMAN
American

Ruin—Torrecilla

1982

colored pencils,
black-and-white photograph

YOU

CAN'T

TEST

COURAGE

CAUTIOUSLY.

ANNIE DILLARD, B. 1945
AMERICAN WRITER

COURAGE IS THE LADDER ON WHICH ALL THE OTHER VIRTUES MOUNT.

CLARE BOOTH LUCE (1903–1987)
AMERICAN PLAYWRIGHT AND DIPLOMAT

CHANCE

IS THE

FIRST

STEP

YOU TAKE,

LUCK

IS WHAT

COMES

AFTERWARD.

AMY TAN, B. 1952
AMERICAN WRITER

Queen Minnie

1986

pastel on paper

. . . YOU CAN
REGARD LIFE
AS A GAME
OF CHANCE.
YOU CAN
PLAY IT
LIKE THAT,
LETTING
THE CURRENTS
CARRY YOU,
OR YOU CAN
WAIT FOR THE
RIGHT CURRENT
AND THEN
PADDLE
FURIOUSLY
WITH IT. . . .

ROSIE THOMAS
20TH-CENTURY ENGLISH WRITER

ONE OF THE MARVELS OF PERSONALITY

IS ITS RESISTANCE TO PREDICTION.

ONE MAN'S PARALYZING TRAUMA IS ANOTHER

MAN'S INVITATION TO TAKE CONTROL OF HIS LIFE;

ONE WOMAN'S GROUNDS FOR INSANITY

IS ANOTHER WOMAN'S GOAD TO

A DRAMATIC SHAPING OF THE SELF.

ROSELLEN BROWN, B. 1939
AMERICAN WRITER

EXPERIENCE

ISN'T

INTERESTING

TILL IT

BEGINS

TO REPEAT

ITSELF—

IN FACT,

TILL IT

DOES,

IT HARDLY

IS EXPERIENCE.

ELIZABETH BOWEN (1899–1973)
IRISH-BORN ENGLISH WRITER

TOBY SCHMIDT

American

Masquerade Series #1

1984

acrylic on quilted linen

WITH AGE AND EXPERIENCE . . . GROWTH

BECOMES A CONSCIOUS, RECOGNIZED PROCESS.

THOSE LONG PERIODS WHEN SOMETHING

INSIDE OURSELVES SEEMS TO BE WAITING,

HOLDING ITS BREATH, UNSURE ABOUT

WHAT THE NEXT STEP SHOULD BE,

EVENTUALLY BECOME THE PERIODS WE

WAIT FOR, FOR IT IS IN THOSE PERIODS THAT

WE REALIZE WE ARE BEING PREPARED

FOR THE NEXT PHASE OF OUR LIFE

AND THAT, IN ALL POSSIBILITY,

A NEW LEVEL OF EXPERIENCE

IS ABOUT TO BE REVEALED.

ALICE WALKER, B. 1944
AFRICAN-AMERICAN WRITER

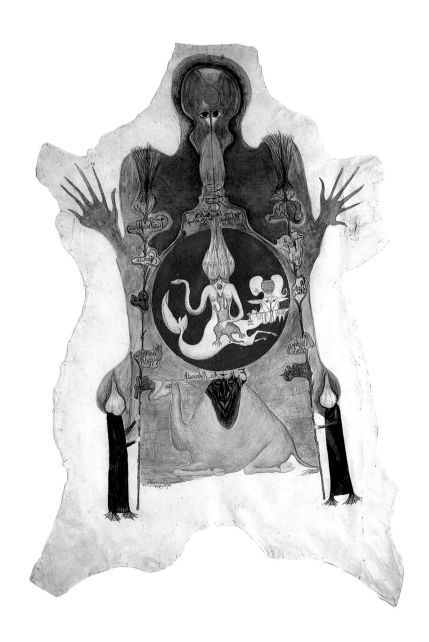

The Magic Witch

1975

gouache on vellum

BETTER

LATE

THAN

NEVER,

TO LEARN

YOU WERE

DESIRED

IN YOUTH.

GRACE PALEY, B. 1922
AMERICAN WRITER

THE SUREST WAY TO MAKE IT HARD

FOR CHILDREN IS TO MAKE IT EASY FOR THEM.

ELEANOR ROOSEVELT (1884–1962)
AMERICAN FIRST LADY, DIPLOMAT, AND WRITER

THERE

IS A

JOKE

THAT

THE REASON

GRANDKIDS

AND

GRANDPARENTS

GET ALONG

SO WELL

IS THAT

THEY HAVE

A COMMON

ENEMY.

CAROL BURNETT, B. 1933
AMERICAN COMEDIAN

MARY H. McFARLANE

American

Schmoo-Machine on a Moonless Night

1982

watercolor

THE TRICK FOR GROWN-UPS IS TO MAKE THE EFFORT

TO RECAPTURE WHAT WE KNEW AUTOMATICALLY AS CHILDREN.

CAROL LAWRENCE, B. 1932
AMERICAN ACTRESS

. . . ONE'S SISTER

IS A PART OF

ONE'S ESSENTIAL SELF,

AN ETERNAL PRESENCE

OF ONE'S HEART AND SOUL AND MEMORY.

Susan Cahill, b. 1940
American Writer

WHAT
WE REMEMBER
FROM
CHILDHOOD
WE REMEMBER
FOREVER —
PERMANENT
GHOSTS,
STAMPED,
IMPRINTED,
ETERNALLY
SEEN.

CYNTHIA OZICK, B. 1931
AMERICAN WRITER

AGNES TAIT

American

Skating in Central Park

1934

oil

M Y DAUGHTER IS EXCESSIVE IN HER SMALL AGE,

TAKES IN THE WORLD LIKE BREAKFAST. . . .

HELEN CHASE
20TH-CENTURY AMERICAN POET

Cantaloupe

1991

oil on panel

. . . HER LIFE AT 13 LOOKS LIKE SOMETHING THAT'S JUST

HAPPENING, UNLESS YOU SEE HER

STANDING OVER IT, DELICATELY CLAWING IT OPEN.

SHARON OLDS, B. 1942
AMERICAN POET

I SEE HOW LIKE A SUMMER FRUIT

SHE RIPENS, AND WONDER,

WILL SHE DROP EASILY TO THE

FIRST HAND THAT REACHES,

OR HOLD FAST, CLINGING TO THE VINE . . . ?

SYDNEY DALEN
20TH-CENTURY AMERICAN WRITER

NOTHING

TAKES

THE

PLACE

OF THE

MOTHER.

ANNIE POTTS
20TH-CENTURY AMERICAN ACTRESS

ELLEN DAY HALE

American

June

ca. 1905

oil on canvas

A MOTHER'S HARDEST TO FORGIVE.

LIFE IS THE FRUIT SHE LONGS TO HAND YOU,

RIPE ON A PLATE. AND WHILE YOU LIVE,

RELENTLESSLY SHE UNDERSTANDS YOU.

PHYLLIS MCGINLEY (1905–1978)
AMERICAN POET

. . . MY KITCHEN
IS WHERE
EVERYBODY
CONGREGATES,
FOR HUMAN
BEINGS ARE
HEAT-SEEKING
CREATURES,
AND THE
KITCHEN
IS THE
HEARTH.
IF A
HOUSE
CAN BE
COMPARED
TO A BODY,
THE KITCHEN
IS THE HEART
OF THE
MATTER.

PHYLLIS THEROUX, B. 1939
AMERICAN WRITER

FROM YOUR

PARENTS

YOU LEARN

LOVE

AND

LAUGHTER

AND HOW

TO PUT

ONE FOOT

IN FRONT

OF THE

OTHER.

BUT WHEN

BOOKS

ARE

OPENED

YOU DISCOVER

THAT YOU

HAVE WINGS.

HELEN HAYES, B. 1900
AMERICAN ACTRESS

Stripes and Peonies

1990

oil on linen

A WORK OF ART IS LIKE A DREAM

WHERE ALL THE CHARACTERS,

NO MATTER WHAT DISGUISE,

ARE PART OF THE DREAMER.

MARISOL, B. 1930
FRENCH-BORN VENEZUELAN SCULPTOR

M A R Y   H .   M c F A R L A N E

American

The Jungle

1982

oil

TRUE

REVOLUTIONS

IN ART

RESTORE

MORE

THAN

THEY

DESTROY.

LOUISE BOGAN (1898–1970)
AMERICAN POET

IF . . . IT MAKES MY WHOLE BODY

SO COLD NO FIRE CAN WARM ME,

I KNOW THAT IS POETRY.

EMILY DICKINSON (1830–1886)
AMERICAN POET

THE

HEART

IS SO

EASILY

MOCKED,

BELIEVING

THAT

THE SUN

CAN RISE

TWICE

OR THAT

ROSES

BLOOM

BECAUSE

WE WANT

THEM TO.

JEANETTE WINTERSON, B. 1959
ENGLISH WRITER

*Roses, Convolvulus, Poppies and Other
Flowers in an Urn on a Stone Ledge*

ca. 1745

oil on canvas

I HAVE THREE PHOBIAS WHICH,

COULD I MUTE THEM, WOULD

MAKE MY LIFE SLICK AS A SONNET,

BUT AS DULL AS DITCH WATER:

I HATE TO GO TO BED, I HATE TO

GET UP, AND I HATE TO BE ALONE.

TALLULAH BANKHEAD (1903–1968)
AMERICAN ACTRESS

IF NEUROTIC

IS WANTING

TWO MUTUALLY

EXCLUSIVE THINGS

AT ONE

AND THE

SAME TIME, THEN

I'M NEUROTIC

AS HELL.

I'LL BE

FLYING

BACK

AND FORTH

BETWEEN

ONE MUTUALLY

EXCLUSIVE

THING

AND ANOTHER

FOR THE

REST

OF MY DAYS.

SYLVIA PLATH (1932–1963)
AMERICAN WRITER

THERE'S
SO MUCH
WE DON'T
CONTROL
IN LIFE,
AND
THAT CAN
BE A KIND
OF COMFORT
CHAOS
IS
BASICALLY
THE STATE
OF THINGS.

GLENN CLOSE, B. 1947
AMERICAN ACTRESS

Figure Posed

1986

pastel

MAYBE

IT WAS

POSSIBLE

TO GIVE

UP CONTROL,

ONCE

IN A

WHILE.

MAYBE

ONE COULD

GIVE UP

CONTROL

AND THE

WORLD

WOULDN'T

FALL

APART.

MARILYN FRENCH, B. 1929
AMERICAN WRITER

MARY H. McFARLANE

American

The Treadmill

1982

acrylic

So what do you do when that spinning starts

and the motion carries the time wild

by you and you cannot stop to see

one thing to grab and stop yourself?

You stand still the best you can

and say strong and loud

for the circle of spinning to stop

so you can walk away from the noise.

Kaye Gibbons, b. 1960
American Writer

I SEEM

TO HAVE

AN AWFUL

LOT

OF PEOPLE

INSIDE

OF ME.

EDITH EVANS (1894–1962)
ENGLISH ACTRESS

[SHE HAS]

STOPPED

IMAGINING

OTHER LIVES;

IF SHE

COULD,

SHE'D

LIVE

THIS ONE

FOREVER.

FRANCINE PROSE, B. 1947
AMERICAN WRITER

MARISOL

French-born Venezuelan

Self-Portrait

1961–2

mixed media

THERE ARE ALWAYS, IN EACH OF US,

THESE TWO: THE ONE WHO STAYS,

THE ONE WHO GOES AWAY. . .

ELEANOR WILNER, B. 1937
AMERICAN POET

AFTER

THE

FEET

OF

BEAUTY

FLY

MY

OWN.

EDNA ST. VINCENT MILLAY (1892–1952)
AMERICAN POET

How can

I ever

know

whether

or not

I'm really

happy

here

unless

I go

somewhere

else?

Cynthia Rich
20th-Century American Writer

ALBERTA CIFOLELLI

American

Litmarsh II

1982

acrylic and pastel on canvas

I CAN'T TREAD GROUND THAT IS ALREADY FAMILIAR TO ME.

MIRELLA RICCIARDI, B. 1931
AFRICAN PHOTOGRAPHER

GABRIELLE MUNTER

German

Staffelsee in Autumn

1923

oil on board

TEMPTATION

TO FLEE

INTO SOME

SORT OF

SIMPLIFYING

THEORY

IS A VERY

OLD

TEMPTATION.

MARTHA NUSSBAUM
20TH-CENTURY PHILOSOPHY PROFESSO

THERE ARE NO SHORTCUTS

TO ANYPLACE WORTH GOING.

BEVERLY SILLS, B. 1929
AMERICAN OPERA SINGER AND DIRECTOR

NEVER CONFUSE MOVEMENT WITH ACTION.

BILLIE JEAN KING, B. 1943
AMERICAN TENNIS PRO

SUSAN TUNICK

American

Rock Salt and Nails #2

1983

oil and acrylic

WE DON'T KNOW WHO WE ARE

UNTIL WE SEE WHAT WE CAN DO.

MARTHA GRIMES
20TH-CENTURY AMERICAN WRITER

. . . THE

MORE

YOU

DO,

THE

MORE

YOU

CAN

DO.

SALLY FIELD, B. 1946
AMERICAN ACTRESS AND PRODUCER

I BELIEVE

THAT LIFE

SHOULD BE

LIVED

SO VIVIDLY

AND SO

INTENSELY

THAT

THOUGHTS

OF ANOTHER

LIFE, OR OF

A LONGER

LIFE,

ARE NOT

NECESSARY.

MARJORY STONEMAN DOUGLAS, B. 1890
AMERICAN CONSERVATIONIST

Electric Prisms

1914

oil on canvas

WHATEVER BELONGS TO THE ORDER OF LIFE

SEEMS TO ME BEAUTIFUL AND RIGHT.

George Sand [Amandine A. L. Dupin] (1804–1876)
French writer

Illustration from *Dissertation in Insect
Generations and Metamorphosis in Surinam*, Plate 1

1719

hand-colored engraving

I WANT REAL THINGS—

MUSIC THAT MAKES HOLES IN THE SKY.

GEORGIA O'KEEFFE (1887–1986)
AMERICAN ARTIST

IN ALL

THAT

I VALUE

THERE

IS A

CORE

OF MYSTERY.

MARGE PIERCY, B. 1936
AMERICAN POET

... ORDINARY LIVES ARE EXTRAORDINARY,

IF YOU REALLY SEE THEM.

AGNES DE MILLE, B. 1905
AMERICAN DANCER AND CHOREOGRAPHER

Collage #17

1975

collage

LIFE'S

NOT ABOUT

THE DAY

WHEN YOU

WIN THE PRIZES—

IT'S ABOUT

ALL THE

DAYS IN

BETWEEN.

SUSAN HOWATCH, B. 1940
ENGLISH WRITER

WHETHER OR NOT WE FIND WHAT WE ARE SEEKING

IS IDLE, BIOLOGICALLY SPEAKING.

EDNA ST. VINCENT MILLAY (1892–1952)
AMERICAN POET

YOU

CAN

THINK

CLEARLY

ONLY

WITH

YOUR

CLOTHES

ON.

MARGARET ATWOOD, B. 1939
CANADIAN WRITER

Nude Doing Her Hair

ca. 1916

oil on canvasboard

A CURVED LINE IS THE LOVELIEST

DISTANCE BETWEEN TWO POINTS.

MAE WEST (1892–1980)
AMERICAN ACTRESS

ELIZABETH OSBORNE

American

Untitled Nude Reclining

1989

oil on linen

A KISS

CAN BE

A COMMA,

A QUESTION

MARK

OR AN

EXCLAMATION

POINT.

THAT'S

BASIC

SPELLING

THAT

EVERY

WOMAN

OUGHT

TO KNOW.

MISTINGUETT (1873–1956)
FRENCH DANCER AND SINGER

. . . STOLEN KISSES ARE THAT MUCH SWEETER

BECAUSE THEY ARE A BORROWED LUXURY.

Sydney Dalen
20th-Century American Writer

TO KISS

WELL

ONE MUST

KISS

SOLELY. . .

PASSION

IS SWEETER

SPLIT

STRAND

BY

STRAND.

JEANETTE WINTERSON, B. 1959
ENGLISH WRITER

LILLY MARTIN SPENCER

American

*Still Life with Watermelon,
Pears, and Grapes*

n.d.

oil on canvas

YOUR HAND FOUND MINE.

LIFE RUSHED TO MY FINGERS . . .

ANNE SEXTON (1928–1974)
AMERICAN POET

I'M

GIVING

UP SWEET

AND

BECOMING

A CREATURE

OF PASSION,

A WILD

THING

THAT

NOBODY

CAN EVER

FULLY

POSSESS.

JUDITH VIORST, B. 1931
AMERICAN WRITER

WHEN I WAS WILD I WAS WILD.

WHEN I WAS A LADY IN LATER YEARS,

I TRIED TO BE A LADY.

MARTHA GRAHAM (1895–1991)
AMERICAN DANCER AND CHOREOGRAPHER

ELISSA DORFMAN

American

Sideview Realistic and
Expansion, Yellow Background

1977

oil

. . . THERE'S

A PLACE

WHERE

HIS

FANTASY

AND MINE

COME

TOGETHER.

HANNA SCHYGULLA, B. 1943
POLISH ACTRESS

Nude in Pink and Green

1979

colored pencils,
black-and-white photograph

HERE UNDER THE SHOCK OF LOVE, I AM OPEN

TO YOU . . .

MAY SARTON, B. 1912
AMERICAN POET

. . . I COME APART

IN YOUR HANDS

LIKE PIECES OF A VAST

AND UNSOLVED PUZZLE.

LINDA PASTAN, B. 1932
AMERICAN POET

I WISH YOU TO KNOW ME NOW

NOT FOR MY BECOMING

BUT MY BEING...

EVE MERRIAM, B. 1916
AMERICAN POET

MARIE LAURENCIN

French

Portrait of Mademoiselle Chanel

n.d.

medium unknown

THERE

IS ONE

LIKE HIM

IN EVERY

WOMAN'S

LIFE, A MAN

WHO

DOESN'T

QUITE FIT,

LIKE

A SHOE

THAT

GIVES

YOU BLISTERS

NO MATTER

HOW

HARD

YOU TRY

TO

STRETCH IT.

IF SHE'S

LUCKY.

EVELYN WILDE MAYERSON, B. 1935
AMERICAN WRITER

IF SOMEBODY MAKES ME LAUGH, I'M HIS SLAVE FOR LIFE.

BETTE MIDLER, B. 1945
AMERICAN ACTRESS AND SINGER

I KNOW
BORING
MEN ARE
THE ONES
TO GO FOR,
BUT ALL
I CAN SEE
IS THE
LIGHT
GLINTING
OFF THE
INTERESTING
ONES.

CARRIE FISHER, B. 1956
AMERICAN ACTRESS AND WRITER

JANE WILSON
American

Waiting Moon

1991

oil on linen

A SUCCESSFUL MARRIAGE REQUIRES

FALLING IN LOVE MANY TIMES,

ALWAYS WITH THE SAME PERSON.

MIGNON MCLAUGHLIN
20TH-CENTURY AMERICAN WRITER

LUCIA SALEMME

American

Shooting Stars

1983

oil on linen canvas

BUT MOST OF ALL IS THE WAY YOU LOVED ME, LOVED ME LIKE I WANT TO

LOVE AND RARELY CAN.

ELLEN BASS, B. 1947
AMERICAN POET

AFTER

A FEW

YEARS

OF MARRIAGE

A MAN

CAN LOOK

RIGHT

AT A WOMAN

WITHOUT

SEEING

HER AND

A WOMAN

CAN SEE

RIGHT

THROUGH

A MAN

WITHOUT

LOOKING

AT HIM.

HELEN ROWLAND (1875–1950)
AMERICAN JOURNALIST

A MAN

IN LOVE

IS INCOMPLETE

UNTIL

HE IS

MARRIED.

THEN

HE'S FINISHED.

ZSA ZSA GABOR
20TH-CENTURY HUNGARIAN ACTRESS

BERTHA LEONARD

American

Lady with her Motherwell

1991

oil on board

YOU SEE
AN AWFUL
LOT OF
SMART GUYS
WITH DUMB
WOMEN,
BUT YOU
HARDLY
EVER SEE
A SMART
WOMAN
WITH
A DUMB
GUY.

ERICA JONG, B. 1942
AMERICAN WRITER AND POET

CAN'T I LOVE WHAT I CRITICIZE?

TONI MORRISON, B. 1931
AMERICAN WRITER AND EDUCATOR

IT WAS AN UNSPOKEN PLEASURE,

THAT HAVING COME TOGETHER

SO MANY YEARS,

RUINED SO MUCH AND REPAIRED

A LITTLE, WE HAD ENDURED.

LILLIAN HELLMAN (1906–1984)
AMERICAN PLAYWRIGHT

FLORENCE BARRY

American

April

1981

acrylic on canvas

ONENESS

IS BLISS.

SEPARATION

IS DANGEROUS.

AND YET

WE PULL

AND PULL

AND PULL

AWAY.

FOR

THE NEED

TO BECOME

A SEPARATE

SELF

IS AS

URGENT

AS THE

YEARNING

TO MERGE

FOREVER.

JUDITH VIORST, B. 1931
AMERICAN WRITER

BEA SAGAR

American

Madonna, Madonna, Madonna

1988

oil on canvas

LIFE IS A DUET.

EVE MERRIAM, B. 1916
AMERICAN POET

KEEP

THE OTHER

PERSON'S

WELL-BEING

IN MIND

WHEN

YOU FEEL

AN ATTACK

OF

SOUL-PURGING

TRUTH

COMING ON.

BETTY WHITE, B. 1922
AMERICAN ACTRESS

TO KEEP

SOMETHING,

YOU MUST

TAKE CARE

OF IT.

MORE,

YOU MUST

UNDERSTAND

JUST WHAT

SORT OF

CARE

IT REQUIRES.

DOROTHY PARKER (1893–1967)
AMERICAN WRITER AND HUMORIST

ROSE NAFTULIN

American

Path through Hollyhocks

1991

oil on linen

To

BE A GOOD

HUMAN

BEING

IS TO

HAVE

A KIND

OF OPENNESS

TO THE

WORLD,

AN ABILITY

TO TRUST

UNCERTAIN

THINGS

BEYOND

YOUR

CONTROL.

MARTHA NUSSBAUM
20TH-CENTURY PHILOSOPHY PROFESSO

THE ONLY TIME I LIKE POWER

IS IF IT CREATES OPPORTUNITIES.

BILLIE JEAN KING, B. 1943
AMERICAN TENNIS PRO

WE

HAVE

LEARNED

THAT

CHANGE

IS A

CONSTANT.

MAGGIE KUHN, B. 1905
AMERICAN CIVIC ACTIVIST

LEE KRASNER

American

Composition

1943

oil on canvas

SIMPLICITY IS THE MOST DIFFICULT THING TO SECURE IN THIS WORLD;

IT IS THE LAST LIMIT OF EXPERIENCE AND THE LAST EFFORT OF GENIUS.

GEORGE SAND [AMANDINE A.L. DUPIN] (1804–1876)
FRENCH WRITER

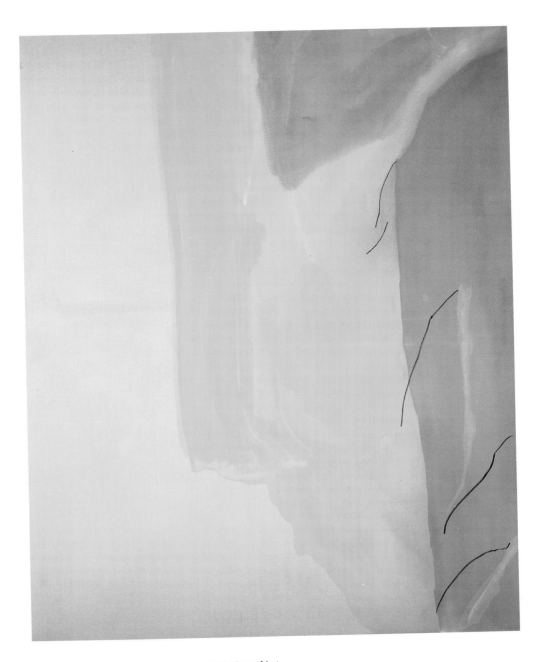

Spiritualist

1973

acrylic on canvas

YOU CAN'T HAVE EVERYTHING. WHERE WOULD YOU PUT IT?

ANN LANDERS, B. 1918
AMERICAN COLUMNIST

TRUTH

IS SUCH

A RARE

THING,

IT IS

DELIGHTFUL

TO TELL IT.

EMILY DICKINSON (1830–1886)
AMERICAN POET

I

DISCOVERED

THAT

I AM

AS BEAUTIFUL

AS I ALLOW

MYSELF

TO BE.

DEBORAH EDLER BROWN
20TH-CENTURY AMERICAN WRITER

Personal Appearance

1985

acrylic and paper on paper

SHE

HAD

FOUND

A JEWEL

DOWN

INSIDE

HERSELF

AND

SHE HAD

WANTED

TO WALK

WHERE

PEOPLE

COULD

SEE HER

AND GLEAM

IT AROUND.

ZORA NEALE HURSTON (1891–1960)
AFRICAN-AMERICAN WRITER

WHAT WOULD HAPPEN IF ONE WOMAN

TOLD THE TRUTH ABOUT HER LIFE?

THE WORLD WOULD SPLIT OPEN.

MURIEL RUKEYSER (1913–1980)
AMERICAN POET

CREDITS

MIRIAM SCHAPIRO (Canadian, b. 1923)
The Poet, 1983.
Acrylic and fabric on canvas, 107 × 72 ″.
Courtesy, Bernice Steinbaum Gallery, New York City

URSULA STERNBERG (English, b. 1925)
Julia, 1991.
Oil on canvas, 36 × 51 ″.
Courtesy, Dr. Eugene Abrams.

EDITH SCHALLER (American, b. 1922)
Invocation, 1982.
Marplex, 31 × 10 × 4 ″.
© Edith Schaller / VAGA, New York 1992.

GEORGIA O'KEEFFE (American, 1887–1986)
POPPY, 1927.
Oil on canvas, 30 × 36 ″.
Museum of Fine Arts, St. Petersburg, FL.
Gift of Charles C. and Margaret Stevenson
Henderson, in memory of Jeanne C. Henderson.

IRENE RICE PEREIRA (American, 1907–1971)
Pillar of Fire, 1955.
Oil on canvas, 50 × 30 ″.
Courtesy, André Zarre Gallery, New York City.

BEA SAGAR (American, b. 1930)
Would You Be an Angel?, 1989.
Oil on canvas, 48 × 48 ″.
© Bea Sagar / VAGA, New York 1992.

SUSAN HEADLEY VAN CAMPEN (American, b. 1951)
Black Hollyhocks in Mimi's Glass, 1990.
Watercolor, 15 × 23 ″.
Courtesy, Gross McCleaf Gallery, Philadelphia.

CECILIA BEAUX (American, 1863–1942)
Sita and Sarita, 1893–4.
Oil, .94 × .635 m.
Paris, Musée d'Orsay.
Lauros/Giraudon/Art Resource, N.Y.

ELAINE FRIED DE KOONING (American, 1920–1989)
Bacchus #3, 1978.
Acrylic on canvas, 78 × 50 ″.
The National Museum of Women in the Arts, Gift
of Wallace and Wilhelmina Holladay.

EILEEN GOODMAN (American)
Hydrangea Bouquet, 1990.
Watercolor, 40 × 26 ″.
Courtesy, Marian Locks Gallery, Philadelphia.

ELISSA DORFMAN (American, b. 1950)
Self-Portrait, 1975.
Oil on canvas, 54 × 42 ″.
© Elissa Dorfman / VAGA, New York 1992.

P. T. FORRESTER (American, b. 1940)
Heavy Heads, 1991.
Watercolor, 40 × 60 ″.
Courtesy, Fischbach Gallery, New York City.

ELAINE NORMAN (American, b. 1950)
Ruin—Torrecilla, 1982.
Colored pencils, black-and-white photograph,
12 1/2 × 8 1/4 ″.
© Elaine Norman / VAGA, New York 1992.

ANNE BOURASSA (American, b. 1948)
Queen Minnie, 1986.
Pastel on paper, 37 × 55 ".
Courtesy, Gross McCleaf Gallery, Philadelphia.

TOBY SCHMIDT (American, b. 1943)
Masquerade Series #1, 1984.
Acrylic on quilted linen, 60 × 60 ".
Used by permission of the artist.

LEONORA CARRINGTON (English, b. 1917)
The Magic Witch, 1975.
Gouache on vellum, 47 3/4 × 32 3/8 ".
The National Museum of Women in the Arts, Gift
of Wallace and Wilhelmina Holladay.
Copyright 1992 Leonora Carrington/ARS, N.Y.

MARY H. McFARLANE (American, b. 1954)
Schmoo-Machine on a Moonless Night, 1982.
Watercolor, 22 × 28 ".
© Mary H. McFarlane / VAGA, New York 1992.

AGNES TAIT (American, 1894–1981)
Skating in Central Park, 1934.
Oil, 33 7/8 × 48 1/8 ".
National Museum of American Art, Smithsonian
Institution/Art Resource, N.Y.

ELLEN HUTCHINSON (American, b. 1948)
Cantaloupe, 1991.
Oil on panel, 27 1/2 × 27 1/2 ".
Courtesy, Gross McCleaf Gallery, Philadelphia.

ELLEN DAY HALE (American, 1855–1940)
June, ca. 1905.
Oil on canvas, 24 × 18 1/8 ".
The National Museum of Women in the Arts, Gift
of Wallace and Wilhelmina Holladay.

PHYLLIS BERMAN (American, b. 1951)
Stripes and Peonies, 1990.
Oil on linen, 60 × 48 ".
Courtesy, Marian Locks Gallery, Philadelphia.

MARY H. McFARLANE (American, b. 1954)
The Jungle, 1982.
Oil, 4 × 5 ".
© Mary H. McFarlane / VAGA, New York 1992.

RACHEL RUYSCH (Dutch, 1664–1750)
*Roses, Convolvulus, Poppies and Other Flowers in
an Urn on a Stone Ledge*, ca. 1745.
Oil on canvas, 42 1/2 × 33 ".
The National Museum of Women in the Arts, Gift
of Wallace and Wilhelmina Holladay.

VAL ROSSMAN (American, b. 1951)
Figure Posed, 1986.
Pastel, 45 × 30 ".
Courtesy, Gross McCleaf Gallery, Philadelphia.

MARY H. McFARLANE (American, b. 1954)
The Treadmill, 1982.
Acrylic, 3 1/2 × 4 ".
© Mary H. McFarlane / VAGA, New York 1992.

MARISOL (French-born Venezuelan, b. 1930)
Self-Portrait, 1961–62.
Mixed media, 43 1/2 ".
Collection of the Museum of Contemporary Art,
Chicago.
Promised gift of Joseph and Jory Shapiro.
© Marisol / VAGA, New York 1992.

ALBERTA CIFOLELLI (American, b. 1931)
Litmarsh II, 1982.
Acrylic and pastel on canvas, 47 1/2 × 60 ".
© Alberta Cifolelli / VAGA, New York 1992.

GABRIELLE MUNTER (German, 1877–1962)
Staffelsee in Autumn, 1923.
Oil on board, 13 3/4 × 19 1/4 "
The National Museum of Women in the Arts, Gift
of Wallace and Wilhelmina Holladay.

SUSAN TUNICK (American, b. 1946)
Rock Salt and Nails #2, 1983.
Oil and acrylic, 72 1/2 × 46 1/2 ".
Photograph by Peter Mauss.
Used by permission of the artist.

SONIA DELAUNAY (French, 1885–1979)
Electric Prisms, 1914.
Oil on canvas, 2.5 × 2.5m.
Paris, Musée Nationale d'Art Moderne.
Scala/Art Resource, N.Y.
Copyright ARS, N.Y./ ADAGP, Paris.

MARIA SIBYLLA MERIAN (German, 1647–1717)
Illustration from *Dissertation in Insect Generations and Metamorphosis in Surinam*, Plate 1, 1719.
Bound volume of seventy-two hand-colored engravings, 2nd edition. The National Museum of Women in the Arts, Gift of Wallace and Wilhelmina Holladay.

RONNIE ELLIOTT (American, 1910–1982)
Collage #17, 1975.
Collage, 18 × 15 ".
Courtesy, André Zarre Gallery, New York City.

SUZANNE VALADON (French, 1865–1938)
Nude Doing Her Hair, ca. 1916.
Oil on canvasboard, 41 1/4 × 29 5/8 ".
The National Museum of Women in the Arts, Gift of Wallace and Wilhelmina Holladay.

ELIZABETH OSBORNE (American, b. 1936)
Untitled Nude Reclining, 1989.
Oil on linen, 52 × 48 ".
Courtesy, Marian Locks Gallery, Philadelphia.

LILLY MARTIN SPENCER (American, 1822–1902)
Still Life with Watermelon, Pears, and Grapes, n.d.
Oil on canvas, 13 1/8 × 17 1/4 ".
The National Museum of Women in the Arts, Gift of Wallace and Wilhelmina Holladay.

ELISSA DORFMAN (American, b. 1950)
Sideview Realistic and Expansion, Yellow Background, 1977.
Oil, 14 × 10 ".
© Elissa Dorfman / VAGA, New York 1992.

ELAINE NORMAN (American, b. 1950)
Nude in Pink and Green, 1979.
Colored pencils, black-and-white photo, 7 1/4 × 10 3/4 ".
© Elaine Norman / VAGA, New York 1992.

MARIE LAURENCIN (French, 1885–1954)
Portrait of Mademoiselle Chanel, n.d.
Paris, Orangerie.
Scala/Art Resource, N.Y.
Copyright 1992 ARS, N.Y./ADAGP, Paris.

JANE WILSON (American, b. 1924)
Waiting Moon, 1991.
Oil on linen, 18 × 18 ".
Photograph by Plakke/Jacobs.
Courtesy, Fischbach Gallery, New York City.

LUCIA SALEMME (American, b. 1919)
Shooting Stars, 1983.
Oil on linen canvas, 35 × 29 ".
Courtesy, André Zarre Gallery, New York City.

BERTHA LEONARD (American, b. 1928)
Lady with her Motherwell, 1991.
Oil on board, 24 × 28 ".
Courtesy, Gross McCleaf Gallery, Philadelphia.

FLORENCE BARRY (American, b. 1943)
April, 1981.
Acrylic on canvas, 36 × 44 ".
© Florence Barry / VAGA, New York 1992.

BEA SAGAR (American, b. 1930)
Madonna, Madonna, Madonna, 1988.
Oil on canvas, 34 × 34 ".
© Bea Sagar / VAGA, New York 1992.

ROSE NAFTULIN (American, b. 1925)
Path through Hollyhocks, 1991.
Oil on linen, 38 × 42 ".
Courtesy, Gross McCleaf Gallery, Philadelphia.

LEE KRASNER (American, 1908–1984)
Composition, 1943.
Oil on canvas, 30 1/8 × 24 1/4 ".
National Museum of American Art, Smithsonian Institution: Museum purchase/Art Resource, N.Y.

HELEN FRANKENTHALER (American, b. 1928)
Spiritualist, 1973.
Acrylic on canvas, 72 × 60 ".
The National Museum of Women in the Arts, Gift of Wallace and Wilhelmina Holladay.
Copyright Helen Frankenthaler 1992.

MIRIAM SCHAPIRO (Canadian, b. 1923)
Personal Appearance, 1985.
Acrylic and paper on paper, 85 × 77 ".
Collection: Mr. and Mrs. Irvin Arthur.
Courtesy, Bernice Steinbaum Gallery, New York City.